Jack Goes Boating

by

Bob Glaudini

SAMUEL FRENCH

FOUNDED 1830

New York Hollywood London Toronto

SAMUELFRENCH.COM

ISBN 978-0-573-65097-0   Printed in U.S.A.   #12581

IMPORTANT BILLING AND CREDIT REQUIREMENTS

All producers of *JACK GOES BOATING* must give credit to the Author of the Play in all programs distributed in connection with performances of the Play, and in all instances in which the title of the Play appears for the purposes of advertising, publicizing or otherwise exploiting the Play and /or a production. The name of the Author *must* appear on a separate line on which no other name appears, immediately following the title and *must* appear in size of type not less than fifty percent of the size of the title type.

MUSIC NOTE

Licensees are solely responsible for obtaining formal written permission from copyright owners to use copyrighted music in the performance of this play and are strongly cautioned to do so. If no such permission is obtained by the licensee, then the licensee must use only original music that the licensee owns and controls. Licensees are solely responsible and liable for all music clearances and shall indemnify the copyright owners of the play and their licensing agent, Samuel French, Inc., against any costs, expenses, losses and liabilities arising from the use of music by licensees.

JACK GOES BOATING had its world premiered Off-Broadway in March, 2007 at the LAByrinth Theatre Company (Phillip Seymour Hoffman and Jack Ortiz, Artistic Directors; SteveAsher, Executive Director). The scenic designer was David Korins, the costume designer was Mimi O'Donnell, the lighting designer was Japhy Weidman and the composition and sound designer was David Van Tieghem. The Production Stage Manager was Damon A. Arrington, assisted by Kristina Poe. The production was under the direction of Peter Dubois with the following cast:

CONNIE	Beth Cole
JACK	Philip Seymour Hoffman
CLYDE	John Ortiz
LUCY	Daphne Rubin-Vega

CAST

Connie
Jack
Clyde
Lucy

PLACE

New York City

(CLYDE & LUCY'S apartment. JACK and CLYDE. JACK'S hair is in newly developing dreads and or/ braids of his own creation. CLYDE has a handsome haircut and a well-trimmed thin mustache. Both are in limousine-driver black suits. JACK is bundled in a winter coat and scarf. CLYDE studies JACK, waiting for an answer.)

CLYDE. ...I think you should.

JACK. Yeah?

CLYDE. Yeah. I think so.

JACK. What's she do there?

CLYDE. She's the assistant to the embalmer.

JACK. Aw, no...

CLYDE. ...something with the fluids.

JACK. ...no, Aw...

CLYDE. No, man. Lucy's training her to sell grief seminars for Dr. Bob. He's doing a tour of seven states.

JACK. Phone sales?

CLYDE. Yeah.

JACK. Oh... cool.

CLYDE. Yeah, she calls the funeral directors. You want to meet her?

JACK. Yeah.

CLYDE. Yeah. Lucy'll set it up.

JACK. What's her name?

CLYDE. Connie.

JACK. From Constance.

(CLYDE relights a joint. Passes it to JACK.)

    CLYDE. *(Cont'd)* You're off Saturday night, right?
    JACK. Yeah, probably.
    CLYDE. Tell your uncle.
    JACK. What if you have to drive?
    CLYDE. I'm not scheduled.
    JACK. You know how it gets weekends.
    CLYDE. We're working the day, he'll be OK with it.
    JACK. Don't mention why.
    CLYDE. Hey.
    JACK. That it's... y' know... because...
    CLYDE. I won't.
    JACK. ...he won't let it rest.
    CLYDE. Not a word.
    JACK. It's how he is...
    CLYDE. I'll think of something to tell him.
    JACK. OK to hear this again?
    CLYDE. Sure.
    JACK. The tape's getting stretched.

(JACK plays "Rivers of Babylon" on a small portable player.)

    CLYDE. You should go CD.
    JACK. Probably.
    CLYDE. Go high tech.
    JACK. Yeah.

(CLYDE listens. Observes JACK.)

    CLYDE. Turn it down a minute. I want to ask you something.

JACK. Turn it down?
CLYDE. Yeah , a minute.

(JACK turns it down.)

CLYDE. Would you call yourself, a rasta man?
JACK. No.
CLYDE. You thinking of becoming one?
JACK. No.
CLYDE. That's all I wanted to know. Turn it back up, if you want. I just wanted to ask.
JACK. I'm into reggae.
CLYDE. I noticed.
JACK. You like the song?
CLYDE. Some of the words, you know, I don't get, so it's hard to commit.
JACK. "Over I" is a hard one.
CLYDE. "Over I?"
JACK. "Over I." Yeah.
CLYDE. I was thinking to ask.
JACK. I'm into this song.
CLYDE. I know.
JACK. Reggae's mainly positive.
CLYDE. You never talked about it. But... y'know... I thought... y'know... We'll just order something and hang around here Saturday night.
JACK. Yeah.
CLYDE. No biggie.

(CLYDE tokes on the joint. He observes JACK, quietly amused.)

Scene 2

(CLYDE'S and LUCY's apartment. CONNIE, JACK, CLYDE.)

JACK. I'm sorry, y'know...
CONNIE. Yeah...
JACK. ... to hear...
CLYDE. Yeah... In a coma, man.
CONNIE. For about three months.
JACK. To see your Dad like that...

(CLYDE relights the joint. Offers it to CONNIE.)

CONNIE. No, no thanks, I'm fine.

(CLYDE passes the joint to JACK. JACK doesn't take a hit. Puts joint in saucer)

JACK. ... after not seeing him for a while...then...*(To CLYDE.)*...y'know?
CLYDE. Yeah...
CONNIE. In a room for people in comas.
CLYDE. Man...in a coma...
JACK. That'd be...what would that be like...?
CONNIE. The coma nurse said when he gasped for air his body did it in a reactive mode.
JACK. Aw, that's...*(To CLYDE.)*...right?
CLYDE. Yeah...
CONNIE. He said your body reacts when the oxygen is used up, so you gasp for air. Like a dry pump. That's how he put it. He said I should talk it over with the family about what

we wanted to do, if it came to, to...y'know... I was thinking that people in comas hear everything. I was glad when he left, and I was alone with my dad.

JACK. ...a hem...hem...that's good, that he left...because...

CLYDE. Yeah.

CONNIE. I was glad he left.

JACK. Yeah.

CONNIE. He was coming on to me.

JACK. The coma nurse?

CLYDE. Right there?

CONNIE. Yeah.

JACK. Right there in the coma room?

CLYDE. That's fucked up.

CONNIE. He stood close, almost touching me, at one point, in fact, he did touch me, and let his hand stay on my arm without saying anything until my dad gasped. Then he left the coma room. I was relieved because he was coming on to me, and my dad was right there. In a coma, but still...

CLYDE. That's not right.

JACK. No, in the coma room with your dad right there? In a coma, yeah, but still, like you say...

CONNIE. No, I know, y'know...because what they say about people in comas hearing everything.

JACK. ...yeah...I think so...

CONNIE. My dad would not be breathing, not moving, y'know, and then gasp for air like that, and twist his body, y'know, jerk around like, I thought, he wanted to get out of there. So when I was alone with my dad, I told him it's OK to go, that he didn't have to stick around. I told him don't worry, I'd take care of mom. I told him I loved him, that he was a great dad. I told him I was gonna make a lot of money, and take care of my mom, and he was free to take off to heaven. I told him things I probably saw in a movie that I believed for some reason right then when I said it. Two days later, he woke up out of the coma.

CLYDE. Fuck.

JACK. That's...wow...woke up?

CONNIE. ...After three months.

CLYDE. Fuck.

CONNIE. He went back to their apartment at Sunshine Valley Care Facility.

JACK . God, that's...got up from a coma and went home.

CONNIE. He wanted me to get his driver's license back from the manager of the facility. He wanted the keys to the car, because it was his car, he said, and it was his license, so he wanted it back. He talked in a soft voice...like...y'know...I thought he's not really here. He's in like a zombie state. Not like Dawn of the Dead, but a zombie state where you stay around because there's some unfinished business you're responsible for — like taking care of my mom.

JACK. Yeah, your mom, of course...

CONNIE. They were married fifty-two years.

JACK. ...yeah, to make sure she was...

CLYDE. Fifty-two? Unbelievable...I mean, I believe it, but wow, fifty-two years.

CONNIE. Then he fell down in the hallway and hit his head, and then he died.

JACK. God...oh...after waking up...a kind of...

CLYDE. Yeah... coming from a coma, and then...

JACK. Yeah, a kind of miracle, to wake up, and then to...

CLYDE. Yeah...

JACK. ...cuz he wanted to take care of your mom.

CONNIE. She was blind. She couldn't walk, really. She imagined things. She told me a nurse came into her room late at night to beat her. She said a mean nurse came in the middle of the night and beat her on the back. I never saw marks, so I thought, no.

JACK. No, not in a care home.

CONNIE. Then they caught a nurse slapping her.

JACK. Jesus.

CLYDE. She didn't make it up.

CONNIE. No.

CLYDE. That's messed up.

CONNIE. One of the care nurses on the late shift. They fired her.

CLYDE. I should hope they did.

CONNIE. She saw things in the air near the end. She was blind but she'd look in the air like she was seeing them. I don't know what, y'know, she never said. I asked if she was afraid to die and she said, no, but that she'd rather not. The bathroom's back there?

CLYDE. Yeah.

(CONNIE goes.)

JACK. I didn't mean, when I asked about her mom and dad...

CLYDE. She needed to talk about it, I guess.

JACK. I though, y'know, make conversation

CLYDE. Lucy said she talks when she's nervous.

JACK. That's OK, though, she talks, I mean

CLYDE. Yeah. Lucy's been gone a while, right?

JACK. Yeah...

CLYDE. They probably didn't have Chunky Monkey at the deli, so she's on a search.

JACK. Yeah...

(Buzzer.)

CLYDE. Huh? Huh? How many times you think, "Hey, y'know, they been   gone a long time," then, buzz, y'know, they're there, or, you think "I haven't heard from so and so", then, ring — ring, y'know?

JACK. Yeah.

CLYDE. It's hard to explain.

JACK. I don't think you can.

CLYDE. Good point.

(Buzzer.)

CLYDE. A very good point. *(Into intercom.)* Yo!

LUCY. *(Offstage, over intercom.)* Yo!

(CLYDE buzzes — JACK is amused.)

CLYDE. What?

JACK. "Yo's" funny...

(CLYDE opens the door. Waits for LUCY.)

CLYDE. "Yo?"

JACK. Yeah.

CLYDE. "Yo?"

JACK. Yeah.

LUCY. *(Offstage.)* Are you ready for Chunky Monkey?

(LUCY ENTERS, slips out of her jacket and scarf. Crosses the room, smiling. Exhibits a bag containing ice cream.)

LUCY. Chunky Monkey coming up.

Scene 3

(CLYDE and LUCY'S apartment. Later that night. CLYDE tastes coffee.)

CLYDE. Hmmm. I'm tempted to say — *(Interrupts his judgement)* Jack's been gone, I wonder —
LUCY. Come on, five bucks you can't tell.

(Buzzer.)

CLYDE. Ha!

(Door buzzer. CLYDE goes to buzz in JACK.)

CLYDE. *(Into intercom.)* Yo!
JACK. *(O.S., from intercom.)* Yo!
CLYDE. I thought maybe he and Connie ran off. *(Smells coffee, musing)* Is it Kona...? Is it the Hawaiian...?
LUCY. You're suppose to taste it, and say what it is. Not otall around.
CLYDE. My nose has lost its edge. Your nose goes, your taste goes.

(JACK ENTERS. Snow on him.)

JACK. It's snowing.

LUCY. They say, a foot.

CLYDE. Took you some time.

JACK. No cabs.

LUCY. We thought maybe you went off together.

JACK. I offered to drive her but she said it'd be too much trouble. Queens, but I would have.

LUCY. Coffee's ready.

JACK. I should go, y'know, if it's gonna snow like that. Smells good, though. Is that the Sumatra?

LUCY. Yeah.

CLYDE. Sumatra? Indonesia...

JACK. Maybe a cup before I go.

LUCY. Must be an early call, if you kept the limo.

JACK. Four a.m.

LUCY. Damn.

CLYDE. You liked Connie?

JACK. We got along pretty well outside, ahem... She said she'd like...ahem...She'd like to go boating.

CLYDE. Boating?

JACK. Rowing in a boat. She said boating, y'know, to go boating...ahem, ahem...sometime, when it's, hem, when...

LUCY. Have some water.

(JACK drinks some water.)

CLYDE. So what did you say?

JACK. What?

CLYDE. When she said she'd like to go rowing in a boat

— go boating.

JACK. I said, yeah, maybe it'd be fun to go sometime.

LUCY. Rowing in a boat?

JACK. We were talking about summer things.

CLYDE. You made a date for next summer?

JACK. No, I'm not, y'know, like that bad to say let's do something next summer, y'know, like six months from now.

LUCY. No, no, no, we know.

JACK. It started to snow, and it came up, y'know, warm weather, and it got to summer, to go rowing in a boat.

LUCY. She must like you.

JACK. Maybe.

LUCY. Yeah! Because I don't think she feels safe around water.

JACK. She doesn't?

LUCY. No. Dr. Bob was talking about the Family Reaction to Accidental Death — and Connie told us about her little cousin that drowned.

JACK. No, she never said.

LUCY. Yeah! She was at her aunt's, at a family reunion, somewhere in the south, like a family thing, a big reunion along a bayou near her aunt's house, and someone started asking, "Where's little Ricky Jr?"

JACK. Oh, man.

LUCY. Yeah. She was ten, she said, but she's been afraid since then. She said "go boating." I think she liked you.

JACK. We were talking about rowing in a boat. She brought it up. Boating. On a lake when it's warmer. She didn't say she was afraid. I said, yeah but I don't know if I want to go out in a boat.

CLYDE. If you're afraid, it's not a good idea.

JACK. No, I'm not afraid..it's...

CLYDE. No, I know...I meant, in general...

JACK. Yeah.

CLYDE. I told you I'd teach you.

LUCY. He taught me.

CLYDE. You never said you wanted to learn.

LUCY. There's plenty of time before summer. Go ice-skating—

JACK. Well—

LUCY. I'll find out what movies she likes.

CLYDE. Five years ago I told you. I'd teach you to swim.

JACK. You were teaching Lucy, and you said it caused problems teaching people you're close to...so, y'know...then later, you said you'd teach me, I thought, you know...I don't think so.

CLYDE. That was when I first started driving for your uncle. I just met you, so I didn't want to talk about something personal, so when you asked, what's wrong, I said it was the swimming lessons.

JACK. It wasn't the lessons?

CLYDE. No, some other thing.

JACK. I should learn, I guess, in case, y'know, I go boating, but if she's afraid of water..

CLYDE. Yeah, you could help her, y'know, get over the fear.

LUCY. Clyde teaches a tai chi swimming style.

CLYDE. It's basically basic swimming.

LUCY. You can go boating, and not worry about drowning, beacuse, y'know, you can swim.

CLYDE. It could be romantic.

LUCY. They go in Central Park.

JACK. I don't know.

LUCY. They go on the Hudson.

JACK. I'd have to think about it.

CLYDE. By summer, maybe, you'll be going away together for weekends to a lake that rents boats. Go boating at night. In the moonlight. Huh? Under the stars?

JACK. I should learn.

CLYDE. We'll go up to 145th. The pool at Riverbank.

JACK. It's heated?

CLYDE. State of the art. Ozone filtration. Olympic scale. Only two bucks.

JACK. OK.

CLYDE. I'm serious.

JACK. I'm serious.

CLYDE. It'll get me back going. I used to go three, four times a week.

JACK. Good. OK. Yeah. Well. I better go. *(To LUCY.)* I wanted to play this for you. *(To CLYDE.)* You liked it, right?

CLYDE. Yeah.

LUCY. He told me you were into reggae.

JACK. It manifests a positive vibe.

(JACK plays the portable player, "Rivers of Babylon.")

LUCY. Makes me want to manifest some ganja.

JACK. I should go.

LUCY. I have Purple Haze.

CLYDE. Haze is back?

JACK. I should go.

LUCY. The guys up the block have Haze, the second stoop.

(LUCY EXITS.)

CLYDE. *(To JACK.)* Haze?
JACK. I should go because of the snow. Here's the "over I"
part.

(JACK puts on winter jacket, etc.)

JACK. *(Along with song.)* "Over I..."

(The song plays on.)

Scene 4

*(DR. BOB'S. CONNIE struggles to close a deal. LUCY wears a
monitoring head phone. She listens in.)*

CONNIE. Uh-huh. Uh-huh. I'm glad the last seminar
helped. "The difference in the new seminar experience" —
Well, Dr. Bob's not here, right this minute, but I...He's at a ser-
vice.
LUCY. *(Quietly emphatic.)* Credit Card.
CONNIE. "The new seminar experience offers techniques
—" That's right — "violent acts...The pain of sudden deaths—"
I did?
CONNIE. Oh, ah — Mrs. Pendecker? *(To Lucy.)* She went
to get her husband.

(LUCY gives the monitor phone to CONNIE.)

LUCY. I'll talk to him. You listen. It's OK. You're getting the pitch, remember, though, always be closing. Connie, it's all right, you're learning. I'll talk to him. You listen. "Hello, the opening, gimme the credit card, the pitch, blah blah, gimme the credit card..." It's a mantra... *(CONNIE repeats after LUCY.)* Gimme the credit card. Gimme the credit card. *(Into phone.)* Hello Mr. Pendecker.

CONNIE. "Gimme your credit card."

Scene 5

(CLYDE and LUCY'S apartment. LUCY with a cup of coffee. Morning, before work.)

LUCY. *(To CLYDE, offstage.)* It's a sales job. That's the bottom line. After all Dr. Bob's talk about how it helps the grieving family, if you don't close, you don't last. Anytime you want to give up the bathroom is cool with me...

(CLYDE ENTERS.)

CLYDE. I was talking to him Jack.
LUCY. I was talking to you.
CLYDE. I was listening.
LUCY. What'd I say?
CLYDE. You have to fire Connie.
LUCY. I like her, but what's with Jack?
CLYDE. He was upset about a guy on the train eating potato chips, dumping them into his mouth. The stuff falling all over.

LUCY. He needs to hook up. It's time. He's got me and you, and the limo job. That's it.

CLYDE. That's it for me. I got you. Jack's a friend. I drive a limo.

LUCY. You take business classes.

CLYDE. He's talking about the MTA.

LUCY. I love Jack. But Jack's like, I don't know what to call it. What would you say?

CLYDE. I don't know what it is you don't know what to call.

LUCY. It's something.

(She EXITS to the bathroom.)

CLYDE. Maybe it's nothing.

(She RETURNS.)

LUCY. Someone eats potato chips on the train, and it's the end of the world.

CLYDE. He's OK.

LUCY. I'm not saying "life threatening". I'm saying I don't know what to call whatever it is. Connie might be good for him. She's...whatever it is. It would be easier to help it along if she were working there, but... and she needs...whatever it is...I don't know

CLYDE. This is what? This coffee? This is the Sumatra, right?

LUCY. The Kona!

(She EXITS. He picks up unlit joint.)

CLYDE. This is Haze, though.
(Coughs, sings.)
"PURPLE HAZE ALL IN MY BRAIN —
LATELY THINGS DON'T SEEM THE SAME —
ACTIN' FUNNY, — *(Tokes.)*
PURPLE HAZE ALL AROUND
DON'T KNOW IF IM COMIN UP OR DOWN
AM I HAPPY OR IN MISERY?
WHATEVER IT IS, THAT GIRL PUT A SPELL ON ME...

Scene 6

(The pool. JACK and CLYDE in the water.)

CLYDE. Let's go a little deeper.
JACK. Deeper?
CLYDE. You'll still touch. A little deeper. Come on, a little more.

(They walk deeper.)

JACK. It's getting deep.
CLYDE. A little more.
JACK. It's pretty deep.
CLYDE. OK. Try it now.

(JACK ducks in and out.)

CLYDE. *(Cont'd)* That's good, but...Jack. That's good, but go under. Make the bubbles under the water, then come up, take a breath, and go under, bubbles, come up, and get a rhythm go-

ing. Breath, under, bubbles, up.
     JACK. OK.
     CLYDE. You'll get used to it. We'll do it together. Ready. But, it's good. Ready. Breath.

(They take a breath.)

     CLYDE. Under.

(They go under. Make bubbles. JACK resurfaces first.)

     CLYDE. You can keep your eyes open.
     JACK. The goggles leak.
     CLYDE. They should suck around your eyes a little bit. How do they feel?
     JACK. OK.
     CLYDE. They suck around your eyes?
     JACK. Yeah, I think. Yeah.
     CLYDE. See if they leak.
     JACK. They feel tight.
     CLYDE. Go under and see?

(JACK dips his head under. Up, quickly.)

     JACK. They seem OK.
     CLYDE. You don't have to close your eyes, though.
     JACK. OK.
     CLYDE. Look at me when we do it. Ready.

(They do it a couple times.)

CLYDE. You're doing good.
JACK. I can do better.
CLYDE. You're doing good.
JACK. I can do better.

(JACK attempts to do so.)

Scene 7

(DR. BOB's. CONNIE on phone to funeral director.)

CONNIE. The seminar is filling up. Get your partner and let's get this done. Mr. Lopez. I know you want to do it. I can hear it. Get your partner *(She coughs into the handkerchief, winces from pain.)* Fuck. Excuse me. *(Discovers blood.)* I'm fine. Thank you.

(LUCY enters. CONNIE wipes mouth undetected.)

CONNIE. No. I'm going to hold while you get him. *(To Lucy.)* I'm sorry I was late.
LUCY. I need to talk to you when your done.
CONNIE. I'm gonna close Lopez. I know it.
LUCY. Dr. Bob wanted to be here too, but he had to leave.

(CONNIE sits, winces, holds her side.)

LUCY. Are you OK?
CONNIE. I'll be alright. I was attacked. I'm fine.
LUCY. What?

CONNIE. I'm with Lopez and Curtis.

LUCY. You were attacked?

CONNIE. On the subway. *(Coughs, blood. LUCY sees it.)*

LUCY. My god...get off.

CONNIE. *(Adamantly.)* Don't take them from me. I'm going to close!

(CONNIE coughs more blood. LUCY dials her cell phone with out panic. The dialogue overlaps, and is at time, simultaneous.)

CONNIE. *(To client.)* Hi, Mr. Curtis.

LUCY. I need an ambulance. A woman was attacked.

CONNIE. Listen. You're number two in Santa Fe, but guess who's number one and never misses Dr. Bob's seminars? The Gutierrez Brothers. That's right.

LUCY. Yes, she's conscious. She's coughing up a lot of blood. Brooklyn.

CONNIE. I need your credit card number to save your spot...Let's do it now. Get your American Express, sure —

LUCY. 7744 4th. 1-800-Funeral. 1-800-Funeral. F-u-n... never mind that — 1-800-386-3725. Thomas Funeral Home. 7744 7th. At 78th.

(CONNIE bends over in pain. LUCY goes to her. Blood.)

CONNIE. *(Taking down credit card number.)* Uh-huh. 3715.33 OK 992 OK. 5692. Expiration? We'll call to confirm. Thanks. *(To Lucy.)* I closed Lopez. *(Groans in pain.)*

LUCY. Baby, the ambulance is coming.

CONNIE. *(Groans, coughs. Blood.)* I closed.

Scene 8

(Subway tunnel. Loud blasts from warning whistles. Green to orange to red warning light. Bright white light flashes. Loud sound of train.)

Scene 9

(LUCY waits in hospital waiting room. CLYDE ENTERS.)

CLYDE. She's alright?
LUCY. They say she's OK. Thanks for coming.
CLYDE. Lucky I caught some time. Roads are no picnic.

(She takes a call.)

LUCY. Hello. Mr. Kendal, thanks for calling back. Sure. I'll wait, no, I'll wait.
CLYDE. You OK? You sounded pretty worried.
LUCY. I thought it was internal bleeding but it was blood from her nose that bled backwards.
CLYDE. Backwards? Weird.
LUCY. Yeah, backwards into your stomach, like a lot. A ruptured dorsal something. She also has a couple fractured ribs.
CLYDE. But she's OK, I mean...?
LUCY. We can say hello soon.

(CLYDE answers his phone.)

CLYDE. Classic Limousine Service. Yeah. Yeah. A rupture

of the dorsal something in her nose and it bleeds backwards
from there, not forward like usual.

LUCY. *(Phone.)* No, you're worth waiting for. *(Lucy waits
for Kendal to return.)*

CLYDE. Yeah, Lucy said a lot. Gets in your stomach. Weird
huh? A couple broken ribs. OK. *(To LUCY.)* Jack's here.

LUCY. He's coming?

CLYDE. He's here.

LUCY. *(Back to phone.)* No, I'm here. I understand. I'll
hold. *(To CLYDE.)* I thought he had an airport run.

CLYDE. Blizzard condition.

*(LUCY starts to touch him fondly, but is stopped by the phone
    call resuming.)*

LUCY. No problem, we'll talk tomorrow. Well... we're
looking for a coordinator in the Phoenix area. No, tomorrow's
good. Dr. Bob thinks you're the best man. We'd love you to do
it. Yeah, we'll talk tomorrow.

(JACK ENTERS carrying a stuffed toy.)

CLYDE. What do you have?
JACK. It's a koala bear.

(Hands it to CLYDE.)

CLYDE. Authentic Koala Bear.
JACK. She's OK?
LUCY. Terrible, huh?
JACK. She's OK though?

LUCY. They said she'll be fine.
CLYDE. He got her a koala.
LUCY. It's cute.
JACK. Think she'll like it?
LUCY. Sure. I'm gonna see if I can learn anything.

(LUCY EXITS. JACK answers his phone.)

JACK. Classic Limousine Service. The hospital. She's OK. A dorsal something broke. No, the nose. Dorsal, something. Makes it bleed backwards a lot. It happens. Yeah. I got her a Koala bear. A stuffed bear. Koala. They live in Australia. Ko-al-a. *(Spells it.)* K-o-a-l-a. OK. OK. Roger that.

(Puts away phone.)

JACK. I told him about Connie, y'know, that I was coming here. Now he'll be asking all the time when am I seeing her again.
CLYDE. Just, y'know....
JACK. Yeah... I have to get out of there.
CLYDE. Me, too.
JACK. I got the application for the MTA.
CLYDE. Good.
JACK. I think, y'know, the tracks? I don't want to work with the public.
CLYDE. You do that now.
JACK. Not large scale.

(LUCY RETURNS.)

LUCY. We can say hello now.
CLYDE. OK.

(LUCY gets a call.)

LUCY. Hang on. *(Into phone.)* Hi, Dr. Bob. You got my message?

(Moves away to talk.)

LUCY. No, before I could tell her. She closed Lopez, broken ribs, blood and all. I think so, too. *(She walks out of sight.)*

CLYDE. We're on for tomorrow?
JACK. Yeah.
CLYDE. We're going to add the kick board.
JACK. In the deep end?
CLYDE. No, not yet. You've been doing the visualizing?
JACK. Yeah.

(CLYDE'S phone rings.)

CLYDE. Classic Limousine Service. Yes, sir. OK. I'm on my way. *(To JACK.)* My Plaza client wants to take his kid to Serendipity for the hot chocolate sundae.
JACK. I hear they're good there.
CLYDE. Yeah. Where's Lucy?

(CLYDE EXITS the waiting area. JACK remains. The bear in the next chair. They're there alone a moment. CLYDE RE-TURNS.)

CLYDE. Lucy said to go in.
JACK. Go in?
CLYDE. She's on the phone with her boss. I gotta go.

(CLYDE EXITS. JACK finally rises. EXITS.)

Scene 10

(Hospital room. CONNIE in bed.)

JACK. Hi.
CONNIE. I took a beating.
JACK. I brought a friend.
CONNIE. Oh!

(He gives her the bear.)

JACK. A Koala bear.
CONNIE. *(Cuddles it.)* From Australia.
JACK. Yeah... "Authentic Koala."
CONNIE. This is so sweet.
JACK. I'm sorry you got attacked.
CONNIE. Me too...
JACK. The airport's closed so...
CONNIE. You gotta be careful driving.
JACK. Yeah.
CONNIE. I look forward to when winter's over.
JACK. Go boating, maybe, like we talked about. I mean, unless you don't want to.
CONNIE. I'd like to go with you.
JACK. It's not summer for awhile.

CONNIE. It seems forever.

JACK. Yeah.

CONNIE. When you want something.

JACK. It'll come quick though. It happens with the Jets. When my uncle doesn't go, I get the tickets. It's a month away, and next thing, Clyde's saying "are you ready for the Jets?" It's like it's in no time at all, it seems.

CONNIE. It seems far, right this moment.

JACK. We could do something before summer.

CONNIE. OK.

JACK. Maybe, I don't know, dinner, when you're better. Make it a big feast. Just have like too much of everything.

CONNIE. No one has done that for me.

JACK. I hope you're a good eater.

CONNIE. No one has ever cooked for me before —

JACK. ...Mmmm...

CONNIE. ... no one has before.

JACK. Well...a...cooking? I was thinking more like —

CONNIE. No one ever.

JACK. Well, ahem, I thought we'd —

CONNIE. That'd be so nice. Wow, you can cook.

JACK. Yeah, but, I meant, y'know, maybe — No one has cooked for you?

CONNIE. Not a man.

JACK. Yeah... Oh. I was thinking —

CONNIE. Oh!

JACK. Oh. I only have the basement at my uncles...but...

CONNIE. It's OK.

JACK. A kind of hot plate...

CONNIE. No. That's alright. I understand.

JACK. No. I want to, and it...no one's cooked for you — no

man?

CONNIE. No, but I understand.

JACK. No, I want to. I'll ask Clyde and Lucy, y'know, to cook there.

CONNIE. Really? A dinner party?

JACK. Ah, well...

CONNIE. I'll probably get out tomorrow.

JACK. Oh, that's sudden, I mean, to —

CONNIE. No, I don't mean —

JACK. — cook, because —

CONNIE. I wasn't saying...Not cook tomorrow.

JACK. Yeah, because...

CONNIE. They want to watch me tonight, but I'll get out tomorrow, I hope.

JACK. I can pick you up.

CONNIE. You don't work?

JACK. Yeah, but...So, you feel OK?

CONNIE. I'm on drugs.

JACK. Probably.

CONNIE. Someone rubbed up against me...He was like, y'know, I could feel he was, y'know...It was pressing against me...

JACK. Oh, no...That's...

CONNIE. I shouldn't have told you. You'll think of it when you look at me.

JACK. What?

CONNIE. You won't like me now that you know some guy —

JACK. No, no —

CONNIE. It wasn't out.

JACK. No, yeah, oh, no.

CONNIE. I spit in his face.

(LUCY ENTERS.)

>LUCY. Hey....Poor baby. How do you feel?
>CONNIE. OK.
>LUCY. Dr. Bob said come back when you feel you're ready.
>CONNIE. Is he mad at me?
>LUCY. Honey, why would he be mad at you?
>CONNIE. He's not going to fire me?
>LUCY. No. He's mad at the man that attacked you.
>CONNIE. *(Overwhelmed.)* You're all so good to me.

(Awkward moment.)

>JACK. Well, I better go. I should get the limo back.
>LUCY. You take the bridge, you can drop me at Pacific for the R?
>JACK. OK. Yeah.
>LUCY. I'll call you this afternoon. *(To JACK.)* I'll meet you in the waiting room.

(LUCY EXITS.)

>CONNIE. Thanks for my new friend.
>JACK. You think you might want to listen to this song? It's a positive vibe.
>CONNIE. Sure.

*(He puts the cassette player by her. Plays "Rivers of
    Babylon.")*

JACK. Some of the words are hard to get, at first, so, takes a few times. Well, I better get the car back.

(He leaves the room. Song plays.)

Scene 11

(Clyde and Lucy's apartment. JACK and CLYDE in limo
suits. Coffee.)

CLYDE. There's a solution for every situation there's a problem. The situation is you want to cook for Connie. This is something you want to do.

JACK. Yeah.

CLYDE. The problem is you don't know how to cook.

JACK. Yeah.

CLYDE. I don't know how to cook. Lucy doesn't cook. Plenty of people don't know.

JACK. And I don't know.

CLYDE. That's right, so what's the solution? *(Pause.)* The solution is to have Lucy's friend, the cannoli, teach you how to cook a meal.

JACK. Who?

CLYDE. The cannoli. His name is Federic. I call him the cannoli. Someone Lucy knows. He's the assistant to the pastry cook at the Waldorf Astoria. Desserts. But he can cook food, too. He can write out the recipe, then go over it with you, give you a lesson, so you can follow it.

JACK. He'll do it?

CLYDE. He'll do it for Lucy. He also knows wines. He

knows everything about a meal you need to know. What do you think you want to make?

JACK. Chicken?

CLYDE. OK. Be open though.

JACK. Chicken, fish, or beef. Anyone of those.

CLYDE. OK. Maybe not fish, no fish, I think. But be open because he might suggest something else, like a...I don't know, a casserole...just be open. Especially to dessert, I'd think. How much do you want to spend?

JACK. About a hundred and something?

CLYDE. Plus wine. Wine might be thirty right there. It could be one-fifty, to do it right. So say, one-eighty something counting practice meals.

JACK. I guess I should practice it.

CLYDE. Sure, what do you think? Don't let the cannoli get carried away, I mean, don't say you'll buy a lot of cooking equipment, for instance. You can work with what we have, a lot of stuff from when we got married we never used.

JACK. OK.

CLYDE. The cannoli can make a recipe and give you pointers.

JACK. OK.

CLYDE. You're on your own, though, because we don't do any of that. We don't chop or mix or whatever. It's something we don't do. When did you have in mind for the dinner party?

JACK. I was thinking in about a month?

CLYDE. A month?

JACK. About a month from now.

CLYDE. OK. Well, then, that means there's no rush. That's good.

JACK. Is cannoli an actual nickname —

CLYDE. The cannoli.

JACK. I mean, should I call him the cannoli?

CLYDE. No, no, no. Call him Federic. The cannoli is something I call him. It's a story I don't want to go into. You have an exit strategy?

JACK. What do you mean?

CLYDE. In case you change your mind.

JACK. I'm not going to.

CLYDE. What if you do?

JACK. I'm not.

CLYDE. That's good. You're serious. Good. I'll ask Lucy to talk to the cannoli. I don't like him that much, not at all, actually, but he's a good guy, I'm told.

JACK. Why don't you?

CLYDE. What?

JACK. Like him.

(JACK answers his phone.)

JACK. Classic Limousine Service. OK. Air France. OK. OK. OK. Roger, that. *(To CLYDE.)* He's calling you.

(CLYDE'S cell rings.)

CLYDE. Classic Limousine Service. OK. Good. Perfect. OK. Yeah. OK. *(To JACK)* I got a UN pick up to go upstate. To Dia Beacon, that art place. What'd you catch?

JACK. Someone from France.

CLYDE. I was gonna pick up Lucy.

JACK. I can do it. You know, and see Connie.

CLYDE Very good. Two birds, so to speak.

(They put on winter coats, gloves, hats, scarves.)

JACK. I turned in the MTA application. My uncle knows someone might help.

CLYDE. Who?

JACK. Someone who knows someone. One of those guys.

CLYDE. On of those guys, well, you'll get at the top of the pile, at least.

JACK. Yeah.

(They are totally bundled up.)

CLYDE. Jack.

JACK. Yeah.

CLYDE. I want to tell you something I don't want to tell you but I gotta tell you. I think. Yeah. Fuck I gotta. I don't want you to freak.

JACK. Freak?

CLYDE. Yeah. Don't freak.

JACK. OK.

(Pause.)

CLYDE. About Lucy and the cannoli. They had a thing.

JACK. What?

CLYDE. A thing.

JACK. A thing?

CLYDE. Yeah. With the cannoli. That's the deal.

JACK. A thing with the chef?

CLYDE. He's not a chef. He's an assistant. She had a thing with him.

JACK. Oh, no. You mean...

CLYDE. Yeah.

JACK. You just found out?

CLYDE. No. It was when it was the swimming lessons. In that time frame. They would hang out a lot, I knew that, but she told me he was gay. I thought, y'know, a guy into pastries. She told me it was a one time thing. Then we talked it out and got honest. I learned it fucking went on for two years.

JACK. Two years?

CLYDE. Off and on. She said. Two years.

JACK. I don't know if I want this guy to show me any-thing. Maybe the dinner thing can just, y'know...ahem...

CLYDE. Don't go there. I recommended him, didn't I? That should tell you something. I don't like him, but it's no ones fault. Like I said, people tell me he's a good guy. It's over. They don't hang out, or nothing, anymore.

JACK. So that was like five years ago?

CLYDE. Yeah.

JACK. But she came clean, so, like you said, it's...hem, ahem...I mean she wanted to tell you, to be honest, and come clean...

CLYDE. She was on the phone with Dr. Bob, and this time she's telling him something about a big cannoli, she was say-ing, a big, big cannoli, and I was listening. She was going on, a ten inch cannoli, I didn't know what it was at first. Big cannoli. Ten-inch cannoli.

JACK. Aw, man...talking about, y'know, aw...

CLYDE. She was recommending him to cook for some-thing, some funeral thing. She went off on this trip, y'know, about, y'know, a big cannoli — big, big, the way she was say-ing it, y'know certain things I was thinking, anyway —

JACK. Aw...

CLYDE. Never. Never. Ever mention it to Lucy. Ever.

JACK. No, no, of course. It's weird you're telling me now.

CLYDE. Why is it weird?

JACK. It's weird to hear, I guess. Ahem...hem. All of a sudden, for you to come out with it.

CLYDE. It isn't rational, OK?! There's no good time, but I needed to tell you, so...

JACK. Yeah, OK.

CLYDE. I can even recommend him, the cannoli, y'know. Federic! It's in the past. But every time at that time of year, I can act, y'know, I don't know, irrational, fucked up, that's why. I keep it hid, mostly, y'know...I should've told you. You're my fucking friend. I should've but now I've told you. That's the deal. I'm OK with it, almost. I mean it's a thing, I'm human, but, you know...

JACK. I understand now about at the Jets that time.

CLYDE. I know.

JACK. You turned against them.

CLYDE. I know.

JACK. I couldn't believe it. They were gonna make the playoffs.

CLYDE. I almost told you that day, I remember, but I didn't, and I just thought fuck the Jets.

JACK. I had to get up and move. I had to walk away.

CLYDE. I didn't know who to take it out on. You take it out on people you love. It all happened before we were tight. Before I started with your uncle.

JACK. Oh.

CLYDE. What?

JACK. — yeah, a long time ago.

CLYDE. It was already over — for a year, or more, maybe — so she was cool with it, saying, it's in the past. But for me, I had just found out, so it wasn't in no past for me.

It's like the grief thing with Dr. Bob. You don't get over it! Ever. You learn to live with it better. That's his thing. His approach. If you're lucky! I dont even think about it, and then I start felling fucked up, and it's that time of year. I hide it, y'know, because the shit attitude can kill something as well as what caused it. Anyway, I'm saying this...You've never been hooked up with someone long term. You take some fucking shots. Keep it in mind with Connie, if that's the way it goes.

JACK. I couldn't handle it.

CLYDE. If you want to, you can handle it. And as far as stats go, I don't believe in them, but as far as they go, fifty percent of couples, someone betrays the other — and more than once! I found that out, and that's the test. When it's more than once.

JACK. Wait.

CLYDE. What?

JACK. It happened again?

CLYDE. Not again. Well, kind of again. There was this death guy.

JACK. Hem...ahem...

CLYDE. A death guy did seminars with Dr. Bob. He was a hotshot. Lucy would tell me there was this brilliant death guy, she said was a narcissistic megalomaniac, but she said how he was great with the seminars. Some kind of death genius. The wives of the funeral directors used to all want to fuck him. This hotshot grief seminar charismatic death genius fucking asshole. He went to California to start his own grief thing. So nothing went all the way, she says. It's difficult, but I've come to be able to almost live with the knowledge that I'll never know the truth.

JACK. Man, I don't know, if I could live not knowing. I mean, once you're the person —

CLYDE. *(Cutting in.)* You can live! But if Connie, or someone you're with, ever starts saying how fucking vain some man is, how fucking narcissistic, and at the same time she says how charismatic, how brilliant, how philosophical, how carnal, how the women follow him around, and how they all want to fuck him, you watch fucking out. Because she's telling you something.

JACK. Lucy had a thing with him too? A death guy?

CLYDE. She said it didn't go beyond the fantasy point with the death guy. She only kissed him, she said. Once. In the elevator, helping move a body, they kissed in there, that's all, she said. There was only so much she got honest with because she attacked me when I wanted the details. You've never been through anything resembling what I'm telling you?

JACK. No.

CLYDE. If it becomes long term with Connie, and it may not, but if it does, and you decide to stick it out anyway, know that you will have bizarre and vivid images of her in sex acts with someone else, know that they will recur periodically. Probably forever.

JACK. Did Lucy tell you something about Connie I should know?

CLYDE. No. Nothing. You OK?

JACK. Yeah.

CLYDE. Well, thanks.

JACK. Yeah.

CLYDE. I needed to unload that, I guess, y'know? It's a burden. You're OK?

JACK. Yeah. Ahem...hem...

CLYDE. I wanted to tell you a couple years ago, but...anyway...so like with the Jets, it wasn't the Jets, it was me, you know, I love the Jets, you know that. And I love you. You know I love you?

JACK. Yeah.

CLYDE. Anyway. Tomorrow. One o'clock. The deep end.

(THEY EXIT.)

Scene 12

(DR. BOB'S. CONNIE closes a deal.)

CONNIE. — and the expiration? This is great, Mr Richter, because well you know why...That's right. Dr. Bob will be happy to hear that you're on board.

(LUCY ENTERS.)

CONNIE. Richter Family is on board.

LUCY. Call it a day.

CONNIE. I'm on a roll. I might stay.

LUCY. Jack's picking me up. He gonna want to give you a a ride.

(Phone rings. LUCY gives CONNIE a knowing look. EXITS to get coats, etc.)

CONNIE. Dr. Bob Grief Seminars. Hi. Yeah. OK.

(LUCY returns with coats, etc.)

CONNIE. *(To LUCY.)* Did you tell him to call me?

LUCY. Clyde was gonna pick me up, but he caught a client and he said Jack would. My guess is he saw an opportunity to give you a ride.

CONNIE. Really?

LUCY. He has a crush going.

CONNIE. He does?

LUCY. Come on. He's gonna cook dinner for you.

CONNIE. He's on Atlantic already.

LUCY. I told him to honk, and we'd come out.

(They put on winter coats. Scarves, hats, gloves.)

CONNIE. Can I tell you something? Yesterday, I stayed late to get the Eden Brothers confirmation...I don't know if I should tell you.

LUCY. What?

CONNIE. Dr. Bob reached in to look at the confirm card I was holding, and he touched my breast.

LUCY. So?

CONNIE. I had the card in my hand and he reached to look and his hand was right on my breast. Like it stayed.

LUCY. Dr. Bob?

CONNIE. He smiled and said I was doing really good. It was right there.

LUCY. Honey, Dr. Bob's gay.

CONNIE. He has two kids, though, so...

LUCY. It happens, someone marries, then has kids, but they're not really into women. That's Dr. Bob. He's totally gay. He's totally out of the closet.

CONNIE. You said women get crushes.

LUCY. Even when they know he's gay, they do. I don't know why.

CONNIE. You think I imagined it?

LUCY. You've been through a lot, and on guard about men. I am, and nobody attacked me.

CONNIE. It felt like he hit on me.

(They are bundled up.)

LUCY. That shit goes on in funeral homes. I mean. I'm not saying it doesn't. There used to be a grief counselor that women were crazy about. I mean women at grief seminars, directors, wives, a family member of the dead, a widow. A total narcissist — a pig, actually, but really charismatic. He didn't pay me the time a day, then he started paying attention. It was like a spell. I'm not going into it, but I know things can happen. I swear, with Dr. Bob it had to be innocent.

CONNIE. I didn't know how to deal with it.

LUCY. You say "Lay off the merchandise."

CONNIE. So maybe I imagined it?

LUCY. You were attacked so...

CONNIE. I didn't imagine the man on the subway.

LUCY. The man beat you up, honey. No way you imagined it.

(A horn honks.)

LUCY. Sounds like our limo is here.

(They EXIT.)

Scene 13

(CLYDE smokes a joint.)

CLYDE. She's just one of those. Once something happens. Things go on inside the mind. I understand it.

LUCY. *(Offstage.)* This is nice stuff. Where'd you get it?

CLYDE. A music-type executive. How'd she say it happened?

LUCY. *(Offstage.)* She was holding a confirmation card and Dr. Bob reached in to look at it.

CLYDE. That was it?

(LUCY ENTERS in a new, sexy, night time getup, smoking a joint. CLYDE is captivated.)

LUCY. I told you I had a surprise.
CLYDE. Yeah.
LUCY. Yeah.
CLYDE. Yeah.
LUCY. She said he felt her breast.
CLYDE. Old Dr. Bob huh?
LUCY. I told her it had to be innocent.
CLYDE. You think so?
LUCY. Dr. Bob?
CLYDE. So, she made it up?

LUCY. No, but I don't know. Who'll ever know? *(She curls up on the couch seductively.)*

CLYDE. Mmmmm. A mystery. So to get at the truth, to re-create the scene, to determine the possibilites...Say, it's late... She stays to confirm a deal.A snowstorm...Dr. Bob enters, "Hello Connie — working late?"

LUCY. Ah, no, don't...no...it's too weird.

CLYDE. *(Reaching in toward "card.")* "Let me look at your confirmation card. *(Hand on breast.)* Very impressive. You're a closer now. Do you like it here at the mortuary?"

LUCY. Lay off the merchandise.

CLYDE. ah-ha. What'd Dr. Bob do?

LUCY. I told her that's what to say next time.

CLYDE. But what actually happened?

LUCY. She doesn't even know.

(The melody from "Babylon." Stops abruptly.)

LUCY. What?

CLYDE. *(Song's in his head)* I can't get it out of my head.

LUCY. What?

CLYDE. Nothing.

LUCY. "On the rivers of Babylon —"

CLYDE. Don't...

(She sings the words she knows and hums the melody. Takes her time, pauses, and such.)

LUCY. "—where we sat down... the wicked carried us away..." That was Dr. Bob I told to lay off the merchandise.

(Moving in on him.)

LUCY. "Let the words of my mouth and the meditation of my heart be acceptable in your sight, over I."

Scene 14

(Front of building. JACK and CONNIE. It's snowing.)

JACK. I'm not cold.

CONNIE. Me neither. I usually freeze.

JACK. It's dark already.

CONNIE. It seems like it's only two seconds we've been talking.

JACK. Yeah.

CONNIE. Now, we're snow people.

JACK. I like talking to you.

CONNIE. I should invite you up but my place is a total mess. I'm gonna clean it, and invite you up, next time.

JACK. Mine's worse.

CONNIE. I'm usually neat, well not neat, but not disgusting.

JACK. My uncle says it's not sloppy people that screw up in the world.

CONNIE. Yeah...We couldn't find them to screw up if we wanted to.

JACK. *(Amused by her.)* Yeah...and we don't want to.

CONNIE. *(Amused by him)* Yeah.

JACK. Well...

CONNIE. Yeah...guess it's time.

JACK. Well...Maybe a little good-night kiss.
CONNIE. Maybe.
JACK. Nothing overwhelming.
CONNIE. OK.

(They kiss.)

ACT II

Scene 15

(CLYDE and LUCY'S apartment. Buzzer. LUCY ENTERS.)

LUCY. *(On phone.)* He just buzzed. Hang on.

(Into intercom:)

LUCY. Yo!

(From the intercom:)

JACK. *(Offstage; over intercom)* Yo!

(She buzzes him in. Unlocks door.)

LUCY. *(Into phone.)* You want to talk to him? Just the dessert. Pears done a la some way. Hang on.

(JACK ENTERS. A box of cooking utensils.)

JACK. Got some stuff here.
LUCY. *(Proffers phone.)* Clyde.

(He puts the load.)

JACK. *(Into phone.)* Yeah. The carmel pears with figs and brandy walnut sauce. OK. See you then.

(Returns phone.)

LUCY. *(To CLYDE.)* Bye.

JACK. We're meeting at the pool after his class. Try out the kick board.

LUCY. I didn't like it that much. It's good for you, though.

JACK. I'm gonna practice the dessert, if it's OK. Ahem. First time.

LUCY. It went all right with Federic?

JACK. Pretty good. I've been practicing mentally. Like Clyde said about swimming. Visualize perfection. I'm gonna make the dessert, maybe twice, if it's OK

LUCY. No arguments here.

JACK. I'll practise the chops au gratin another time.

LUCY. I'm glad Federic was helpful.

JACK. Yeah, the cannoli was cool.

LUCY. Uh-huh.

JACK. Yeah, ahem, he has a pretty good job, assistant, right, to the pastry cook? Ahem.

(LUCY lights a half-smoked joint.)

LUCY. Mmmm?

JACK. *(Takes joint.)* Maybe lubricate the imagination before creation.

(He imbibes.)

LUCY. You got the nervous thing.

JACK. Mmmm.

LUCY. The thing you thought was throat cancer. "Ahem...

hem..." You're doing it.

JACK. I am?

LUCY. It's what you do when you're nervous, right?

JACK. I might not even know I'm nervous, then my throat thing starts. Cooking, I guess. Maybe. I'm under a lot of pressure.

LUCY. Yeah?

JACK. ...Ahem... If I work for MTA, I don't know, it would be a new thing. That makes me nervous. The idea of that. The thing with Connie, that's a new thing, hoping that goes OK. Cooking. Ahem. Learning to swim. Thinking about boating. Rowing. So many new things. Ahem... em....hem...That could be part of it.

LUCY. What'd Clyde say about the cannoli?

JACK. Who?

LUCY. You called Federic the cannoli.

JACK. Clyde said it was a nickname.

LUCY. Clyde doesn't like him.

JACK. He said he was a good guy, though. Ahem...em...hem...

LUCY. So what else did Clyde say?

JACK. Ahem...hem...hem...

LUCY. Jack?

JACK. What?

LUCY. He told you about the thing with the cannoli, didn't he? It's OK, you know. We worked through it.

JACK. Two years, though, that's what would get me. Y'know, thinking about the two years.

LUCY. I didn't see him that often.

JACK. That's what I couldn't handle, thinking for two years I didn't know what was going on, but maybe sensing something wasn't right, and not knowing, thinking it was me, and that I was paranoid. That's what I couldn't handle. Then finding out. Thinking every little thing that went wrong between us for two years was because you were thinking of seeing the cannoli. I couldn't handle it.

LUCY. Jack. It was five years ago. Relax a little bit.

JACK. I just found out. I'm just talking about what's up with me about it, and I shouldn't.

LUCY. No, that's what friends are for. I'm glad he told you. It was what it was. I got lost. We got through it. What?

JACK. He mentioned a death guy?

LUCY. Who?

JACK. Some guy you worked with...a death guy?

LUCY. He told you that too?

JACK. He said you told him you just kissed the death guy in the elevator, but he didn't know for sure. That's what he said you've got to be able to live with. Not knowing for sure.

LUCY. What else did he tell you?

JACK. Nothing.

LUCY. Yeah, well, there are things he has to deal with too, on his side.

JACK. Ahem. I shouldn't have talked about it.

LUCY. He didn't mention the Poughkeepsie woman he drove to Poughkeepsie before the cannoli? He hooked up with a Poughkeepsie woman. Just once, he said, like that made it OK. I told him about the cannoli and he told me about Poughkeepsie, so then I told him about the death guy, and then he shut up. I guess he didn't mention the Poughkeepsie woman in the back seat while he was telling you all about me.

JACK. I'm sorry.

LUCY. For what?

JACK. I don't know.

LUCY. You've never been in a relationship for any length of time.

JACK. No.

LUCY. A lot happens.

JACK. That's what he said.

LUCY. A lot are good things.

JACK. Yeah.

LUCY. A lot are things you wouldn't wish on your enemy.

JACK. Ahem...em...hem...

LUCY. It's probably good to know this from people you care about and who care about you.

JACK. Yeah.

LUCY. If it becomes something with Connie, I mean, when you stay together with someone, things'll come up that you have to live with.

JACK Ahem...em...Has she told you anything?

LUCY. Don't trip.

JACK. No, no way...

LUCY. It's good for you to see you can go through things and stick it out.

JACK. Yeah.

LUCY. Learn about shit you don't like and live with it.

JACK. Yeah. OK. Well...I better...I'm gonna core the pears. Yeah, it's gonna be good. Caramel pears with figs and brandy-walnut sauce.

LUCY. Sounds good.

JACK. *(Visualizes. Subtle gestures.)* Squeeze lemon. Combine syrup and lemon juice. Perfect. Stir till blended.

(He repeats gestures.)

Scene 16

(Pool deck. CLYDE holds a kickboard. Demonstrates.)

CLYDE. You kick like this, the whole leg, not just the feet, not just from the knees. Like this. Not like this. Not like this. Like this. Let's see you. Right. Like this. Then, breath, like this, breath, head down, like this, kick, kick, kick, kick, breath out, up, like this, keep kicking, breath, kick, kick, kick, down, and so forth. Hold it out like this in front, keep the end up a little like this, and breath in, breath out...kick...kick for the side...kick, kick, kick, kick...Good, good. Head, head, head.

Breath — kick, kick, kick — head down, head down, bubbles, bubbles, kick, kick, like this, like this, not like this, like this, good, good, good, champion, champion, master kick board, champion...Now back, back this way.... good, good, kick, kick, kick, breath out under, breath in up, kick, kick, kick. Bubbles, bubbles, bubbles.

Scene 17

(CONNIE'S place. CONNIE on the bed. Cover pulled up part way. JACK sits on edge of bed.)

CONNIE. You're a good kisser.
JACK. Thanks. Ahem...em...hem...
CONNIE. I'm sorry.
JACK. No...
CONNIE. I'm not ready, yet, for penis penetration.
JACK. Well...um...no...

CONNIE. I want to, but...Physically I'm OK with it.

JACK. No, it's OK. I'm not, y'know an expert, so...

CONNIE. It isn't that. I've even imagined it with you.

JACK. That's...yeah?

CONNIE. Thinking about it with you.

JACK. Oh.

CONNIE. In the bath tub, I imagined I was with you.

JACK. We took a bath?

CONNIE. No, I was in the tub imagining it was pitch black night. We were in bed in a space ship flying through super space.

JACK. That's a long way off. I mean, space travel...for tourists.

CONNIE. You can touch me again if you want. If you want to, like you were. I'm not ready for total intimate contact, yet. I will be with you, though, I can tell, but not yet, and it's not because I don't think you're sexy. You are. I wouldn't imagine being with you out beyond the Milky Way, if I didn't think you were sexy. I like how you touch me. How you barely touch my skin.

JACK. Ahem...em...hem.

(Moves his hand under the cover.)

CONNIE. I listened to your song over and over. I see why you like it. It's sad though.

JACK. Yeah, but it's positive, though. Positive vibe.

CONNIE. "How can we be thinking of a song in a strange land" is so sad.

JACK. "...King Alpha's song."

CONNIE. I thought it was "thinking of a song."

JACK. No. "Sing King Alpha's song."

CONNIE. Oh.

JACK. It takes a while to understand.

CONNIE. That feels good.

JACK. Ahem...em...hem...

CONNIE. You can stop if you...

JACK. I like it.

CONNIE. When we go boating, I'll lay down with you in the grass. I pictured it when we were standing in the snow looking for a cab. I thought of summer and rowing in a boat. I thought of getting out and walking under some trees, finding green grass, with wild flowers, and you taking me in a kind of animal den under branches — and being intimate with you there. I know you haven't said you'd be patient and wait for me to get over my problems. Now that you know I have some.

JACK. I'll wait.

CONNIE. It could be sooner, but I know summer for certain.

JACK. OK.

CONNIE. I love your fingers.

JACK. Thanks.

CONNIE. Can I ask you something?

JACK. Yeah.

CONNIE. What do you want to see in a woman?

JACK. You mean, you...or...?

CONNIE. Yeah, but, y'know when you think of in a woman? What do you want to see in her?

JACK. Someone who likes music... someone positive. Not a dark mood person.

CONNIE. Those are all nice things. Not too hard.

JACK. Sorry, I...

CONNIE. No, I mean, you're being gentle. I mean it's not hard to be a positive person with you.

JACK. Someone who doesn't need to look around to other men.

CONNIE. You mean have sex with other men?

JACK. Yeah, to feel, y'know, when she feels lost or something, she has to.

CONNIE. I won't do it ever.

JACK. What do you want to see?

CONNIE. A sense of humor. A sense he can tell me the truth. Patient, like you. Sexy.

JACK. I could be some of those.

CONNIE. You're all of them.

JACK. I'm sexy.

CONNIE. You are.

JACK. A sense of humor there...

CONNIE. Can I ask you something that's probably stupid not to know, but who's King Alpha?

JACK. King Alpha, he's like a messiah, I guess, to Rasta. A messiah to Almighty God Jah Rastafari.

CONNIE. Then are you a rasta person?

JACK. No, not really. I don't believe in anything, I mean, I believe in what's here, I guess.

Scene 18

(Swim deck. CLYDE demonstrates.)

CLYDE. Thrust and continue. Thrust. The hip drives the thrust. A stabbing thrust, a slicing in, and follow through. Like this. Stab and continue. Stab and continue. Thrust and follow through. Twist your body, slippery, as you stab. Twist as you stab. A stabbing thrust. Slicing in...like this, not like this. Like this. This is the line of the body. Arm along head, arm along side, twist. Like this. No resistance. Eliminate resistance. Slow, from the elbow, trail the fingers along the surface, slow, barely touch, tease the water, and thrust and continue, slow, slow, slow, thrust, slicing in. Slow, slow, thrust. Don't think about bringing it back. Thrust and continue. It'll happen. Yeah, yeah, breath, slow, thrust, breathe out, yeah, yeah, stab and continue.... Along the body. Arm along the body, twisting, twist, slow, stab...slippery... it's about being slippery...and kick like this...on the twist like this...slow, trace lightly, stab, twist, like this...slippery, like this, and the kick, the kick...

Scene 19

*(CLYDE and LUCY'S apartment. JACK waits as LUCY tries
	the chops au gratin.)*

LUCY. Oh, this is really good.
JACK. Really?
LUCY. Oh, yeah.
JACK. It's not too overdone?
LUCY. No...
JACK. Or...
LUCY. No.
JACK. It's a simple dish but...to get it...it's OK? You'd tell me?
LUCY. So good...
JACK. It's not perfect yet but...a little more sauce? *(He serves her more sauce.)*

LUCY. You became a gourmet cook for her. You must really like her.

JACK. Yeah. Pretty much. She's honest about herself. What she thinks, she talks about. About how she feels. About imagining things or not, ah, what men'll do. I wouldn't care if she does, y'know, imagine things, all the things I can think up.

LUCY. Men do a lot of creepy things. Some guy on the street plays air hockey with his tongue, tells you how great he is.

JACK. Aw, man, that's...

LUCY. That shit happens. Mmmm. Good sauce.

JACK. She doesn't want to have sex, yet. She's still, well, messed up, I guess.

LUCY. It'll work out.

JACK. She thinks summer.

LUCY. Clyde said the swimming's going really good.

JACK. I'm not in the deep end, but little by little.

LUCY. He's a maniac, right? "Kick like this, not like this... like this..."

JACK. Yeah. I'm learning though.

LUCY. She eats your chops, au gratin, the dessert, brandy sauce, some fine wine, she's gonna be moved along the path to righteousness.

JACK. I'm going to clean up the kitchen.

LUCY. I'm looking forward to Saturday night.

JACK. It got here fast. My mind-goal is set for perfect. Ahem...em. Praise Jah I and I.

(He takes the plate and EXITS. She eats)

LUCY. Jack? Is there a dessert?

JACK. *(Offstage.)* Coming up?

Scene 20

(Subway platform. Express roars by. CONNIE howls as it passes.)

CONNIE. Ahhhhhhhhhhhhhhhhhhhhhhhhhhhhhhhhhhh ooo-woooooooooyeaaaaaaaaaaaaaaaaaaaaa!

Scene 21

(Carhorn blasts. Traffic sounds. CLYDE behind the wheel.)

CLYDE. Fuck. Fuck. Fuck. Fuck everyone in the world! Fuck! Fuck! Fuck! The whole fucking world!

Scene 22

(JACK'S basement. Ear phones on. Takes hit from bong. Visualizes.)

JACK. Sift flower. Pinch of season salt. Crumbs. Pepper. Combine in brown bag. Crush garlic. Dab chops. Add to bag. Shake. Remove. Set aside. Yeah. Perfect. Wash, chop parsley. Peel, grate leek, set aside. Yeah. Preheat 350. Squeeze lemon. Core pears. Combine syrup, lemon juice. Stir till blended. Dip pears. Set aside. Yeah. Peel. Perfect. Slice. Potatoes. Yeah. Perfect. Butter. Thin layer. Spread. Add onions. Stir. Add pepper, milk, cheese. Layer potatoes. Cover with sauce. Perfect.

Breath. Head under. Breath out. Open wine to breathe. Kick like this. Not like this.

Scene 23

(CLYDE and LUCY'S apartment. CLYDE and LUCY. CLYDE with a glass of wine. JACK in the kitchen.)

LUCY. Don't get weird.

CLYDE. You asked what I was thinking.

LUCY. Don't get drunk.

CLYDE. I know.

LUCY. Jack's happy.

CLYDE. I know.

LUCY. He made the chops six times.

CLYDE. I ate them six times. I don't think I can eat them again. I can't eat the potato thing again.

LUCY. You have to.

CLYDE. I can't eat the dessert thing again, either.

LUCY. You have to. The chops, the potato thing, it's au gratin, by the way, and the dessert too. It means a lot to him.

CLYDE. OK.

LUCY. Forget about Federic.

CLYDE. You brought him up.

LUCY. You recommended him.

CLYDE. I know

LUCY. All I said was Jack did a good job learning to cook. All I said was Jack was a good student.

CLYDE. I don't have trouble with it in reality. It's in my head I have trouble.

LUCY. You're boring with this fucking thing. It's like Jack playing one song to death.

CLYDE. You think I want pictures in my head of you naked in the butter pantry of the Waldorf-Astoria?

LUCY. Don't blame me for the pictures in your distorted mind.

CLYDE. You never told me the details, so I'm forced to imagine them.

(JACK ENTERS.)

JACK. She called from the stop, so... You hungry?

CLYDE. Yeah. It's...I'm very eager. I'm gonna go for a walk around the block to get my appetite going. I'll be right back. Five minutes.

JACK. I'd better open another bottle of wine. Federic said to let it breathe.

CLYDE. That's right, fine wine should breathe. OK. I need some air. Five minutes. Maybe we should invite him, invite the cannoli.

JACK. The cannoli?

CLYDE. Just for dessert.

CLYDE. It could help to have him over and not let it not be a big thing.

JACK. Have the cannoli over?

CLYDE. Just for dessert.

JACK. I know but...

CLYDE. Lucy?

LUCY. Hey, I'm not the one gonna be fucked up by it.

CLYDE. I'm not gonna be. Jack, you gonna be?

JACK. He's not gonna be critical is he? I mean, he's a professional cook.

CLYDE. You told Lucy he was a good teacher, right? Demanding, a little, a little megalomania — but creative, thoughtful.

JACK. Then get more brandy. I have to make a couple more desserts if he does. Good brandy.

CLYDE. I think I have his number from back when I made him a series of calls. Here it is, the big cannoli.

(CLYDE makes a call.)

LUCY. You do this when you drink. You make an ass of yourself.

CLYDE. Whatever. Voice mail. *(Leaving message as he exits.)* Federic. This is Clyde as in Lucy and Clyde. We were hoping you'd come by tonight for dessert and coffee. See how your student did on the brandy walnut sauce — the au gratin...

(CLYDE EXITS.)

JACK He's OK?
LUCY Don't let it spoil the evening.

(Buzzer.)

LUCY. *(Into intercom.)* Yo.
CONNIE. *(Offstage over intercom.)* Yo.

(LUCY buzzes her in.)

LUCY. He's won't come.

JACK. OK.

(Lucy opens door.)

LUCY. Clyde messes up and fucks someone, but that's OK because he's a guy.
JACK. No, well...
LUCY. Yes.
JACK. He said, y'know, he wished he hadn't.
LUCY. "I wish I hadn't." We all got that T shirt in the drawer. *(Upon seeing CONNIE.)* Jack, someone beautiful's here.

(CONNIE ENTERS.)

JACK. OK. Yeah. You look really good.
CONNIE. Thanks.
JACK. Wow, you dressed up.
CONNIE. I shouldn't have, right?
LUCY. You're perfect. I was just about to go dress my best.

(She EXITS.)

CONNIE. Am I too early?
JACK. No, no.
CONNIE. Smells really good.
JACK. You want some wine?
CONNIE. That'd be nice.
JACK. It's French. A French Bordeaux.
CONNIE. I just saw Clyde.
JACK. He went for a walk. He's working up an appetite.

He wants to out-eat everyone, I think.

CONNIE. He's OK, right?

JACK. Yeah he's...

CONNIE. He looked kinda down, but, yeah, when he saw me he smiled and said, "Hot to trot."

JACK. Yeah... He went for a walk, ahem...hem..."hot to trot"?

CONNIE. You know, like a compliment, but he looked, I don't know, a little upset, maybe.

JACK. He went to get his head straight, I think, y'know, get in a more positive vibe.

CONNIE. Yeah, yeah, he gave me a hug even.

JACK. A regular hug, right? I mean, you're not saying...

CONNIE. No, nothing, yeah, regular.

JACK. I think he had a little wine, so —

CONNIE. Y'know, he just said, "Nice cha-chas," and hugged me, and said he'd see me in a minute.

JACK. Oh. OK. He said "Nice cha-chas"

CONNIE. He was trying to, like you said, probably trying to find a good vibe.

JACK. Yeah. He's OK. Wine, coming up.

(Starts to pour. Stops.)

JACK. Um, ahem, he hugged you...I know, but...That's it?

CONNIE. Yeah. It was just, y'know, "Hot to trot," and he hugged me, y'know, and he said, "Mmm, soft, nice cha-chas, see ya later." He's OK though?

JACK. Yeah...soft...he doesn't drink usually, so a little, y'know —?

(LUCY ENTERS. Sexy dress. She carries a colorful, four-person hookah.)

LUCY. See what I have? A brand-new hookah, ready to be broken in.

JACK. Yeah, wow.

CONNIE. I've never tried a hookah.

LUCY. First time for everything, right, Jack?

JACK. You just got it?

LUCY. A special night for special people.

JACK. That's...a hookah...that's something. Connie's having wine. You want a glass?

LUCY Not yet.

CONNIE. You look really pretty. Doesn't she Jack? Sexy.

JACK. Yeah, well... time to take a check on things.

(JACK EXITS. LUCY takes hash from a jewelry box. She massages the hash and loads the hookah.)

LUCY. Time to prime this mystical instrument.

CONNIE. What exactly will we be smoking?

LUCY. Very purple hash. I used to get high with a bagpipe player from Scotland. He could really take a puff.

(LUCY stokes the pipe and takes a big pull. Holds it in.)

LUCY. He'd let it out and say, *(Lets it out, like the Cheshire Cat.)* "Who... are... you?" But with, y'know a brogue?

(LUCY passes a hose to CONNIE. CONNIE puffs on the hookah. JACK ENTERS.)

JACK. The au gratin is turning the required amber hue. A critical juncture. Federic said, "Cooking is timing."

LUCY. Join the christening of the hookah.

CONNIE. *(Exhales; attempts brogue, to JACK.)* "Who... are...you?"

(CLYDE ENTERS with a bottle of brandy.)

CLYDE. Hey, hey, hey. My, my, my...foxy ladies. We're both lucky guys, Jack, lucky guys. Two foxy ladies. Did my foxy lady get a hookah, Jack, for a special night? She did. *(Displaying the bottle.)* And did I get a little after-dinner brandy— a fine cognac — an excellent cognac to go with another after-dinner surprise I have for us? Maybe later to sprinkle a little of the surprise on the hashish. Who knows? *(Gives bottle to JACK.)* A Napolean cognac, Jack, that I have sampled to make sure it was worthy of your walnut sauce.

JACK. Thanks, well, I better...

CLYDE. Hold on a minute, Jack, I want to say something upon this occasion of your dinner party. Jack's a true sweetheart. Someone is a lucky lady, a very foxy lady is a very lucky lady. I want to say, no matter who or what may try in this life to fuck things up, no matter what shit surrounds and threatens to engulf us, we will face it together, and we will not grow bitter.

(He takes a hookah hose. Gives it to JACK.)

CLYDE. Let's smoke a toast with this beautiful hookah my foxy lady got specially for this night. Let's smoke to Jack, master chef. To Jack.

LUCY. To Jack.

CONNIE. To Jack.

(They all take big pulls.)

CLYDE. Ah, yes...
CONNIE. Wow.
JACK. Yeah. Good.
LUCY. *(Brogue.)* "Who...are...you?"
CLYDE. Prime the appetite. Awake the jaded taste buds. To Jack.

(They puff up another hit. Smoke creeps in from the kitchen during the following.)

JACK. This is so cool. Lucy, to get this, so perfect.
LUCY. Thank you, Jack.
JACK. Hash is spiritual.
CONNIE. *(Sniffs.)* What's that?
JACK. What?
CLYDE. *(Sniffs.)* Something's burning? Burning? *(Attempts to smell it.)* I don't — no...

(Smoke alarm goes off in the kitchen.)

JACK. no... *(Rushes into the kitchen. Offstage.)* Oh. Oh... shit. Oh. Oh. no.

(Sound of a pan being tossed. LUCY goes into the kitchen.)

LUCY. *(Offstage)* Clyde!

(Another crash from kitchen.)

    CLYDE. I'm coming, Jack.

(He EXITS to kitchen. LUCY returns to front room, coughing carrying two halves of the broken, charred and smoking casserole dish, stacked one on top of the other.)

    LUCY. *(To CONNIE.)* D.O.A.
    CONNIE. Oh, shit.

    JACK. *(O.S.)* Everything burned. Aw, look at this. Aw... fuck!

(CONNIE bolts for the kitchen. She quickly back pedals. JACK ENTERS from the kitchen, Angered.)

    JACK. Aw..hem...

(JACK sees smoldering pan in LUCY'S hands and EXITS into bathroom.)

    CONNIE. Jack!
    LUCY. Get the door!

(CONNIE opens the door. LUCY EXITS apartment to dump th dish. CONNIE looks in kitchen.)

    CLYDE. *(Offstage.)* Shut the fuck up! Lucy!

(CONNIE immediately goes to the bathroom. Knocks. LUCY

RETURNS and fans the door.)

    CONNIE. Are you alright?
    JACK. No.

(Alarm stops. CLYDE ENTERS.)

    LUCY. Smells like ass in here.

(Alarm begins again. CLYDE RETURNS to the kitchen.)

    CLYDE. *(Offstage.)* Where's that hammer?
    LUCY. Under the sink!
    CLYDE. Where?
    LUCY. *(Exiting to the kitchen.)* The sink.

(CONNIE knocks on bathroom door. LUCY enters spraying air freshener.)

    CONNIE. Jack?
    JACK. *(Offstage.)* Not now, OK?
    CONNIE. I'd like to talk to you.
    JACK. *(Offstage.)* I just need a minute.
    CONNIE. Please.
    JACK. I need a minute!
    CLYDE. *(Offstage.)* Shut up you fucking cocksucker!

(CLYDE ENTERS from the kitchen. He displays the mangled alarm.)

    CLYDE. Solved. Where is he?

CONNIE. The bathroom. He said he needs a minute.

LUCY. *(To CLYDE.)* Talk to him.

CLYDE. He needs a minute.

LUCY. You know how he was when he wrecked the limo. This is ten times worse.

CLYDE. No razor blades in there, right?

(CONNIE makes to bolt at the bathroom door. CLYDE grabs her.)

CLYDE. I'm kidding.

CONNIE. Jack, I love you!

CLYDE. Keep calm.

CONNIE. Are you OK?

CLYDE. It's Jack. OK? Jack. Not just anybody.

LUCY. *(To Connie)* Clyde'll talk to him.

CLYDE. Jack? We can get by this. Everything's ruined, that's fucked up, but we can get by this.

JACK. *(Offstage)* It always happens.

CLYDE. What?

JACK. *(Offstage)* When there's something good.

CLYDE. I can't hear you. Open the door.

JACK. *(Offstage, the door opened a crack)* It happens when there's something good I want.

CLYDE. It fucked up, but it fucked up because we forgot...

JACK. *(Offstage)* I forgot because you made a fucking toast!

CLYDE. Because I love you. We all love you. You forgot because you were being loved, and enjoying yourself. That's the important thing to remember.

JACK. *(Offstage)* The meal was important.

CLYDE. I know. I mean, I don't know, but...

JACK. You don't know. You don't know anything. Go fuck yourself!

CLYDE. Jack...don't be like this, man.

JACK. GO AWAY!

(CLYDE ponders the situation. CONNIE knocks on bathroom door.)

CONNIE. Jack. Don't be upset. Jack

JACK. I'm trying not to be!

CLYDE. Where is the thing?

CONNIE. What thing?

(CLYDE hums the song.)

CLYDE. The thing.

LUCY. Oh!

CONNIE. Yeah.

LUCY and CONNIE. The thing.

CLYDE. JACK!

JACK. I visualized the perfect dinner!

CLYDE. I know how you feel. Things are going good just like you pictured it, and out of the blue -

JACK. It was going to be perfect!

(LUCY returns with the portable player. Gives it to CLYDE.)

CLYDE. I know. But "positive vibes." Who said that? Who said, "positive vibes"? We had positive vibes, enjoying ourselves, then a negative thing came along, and everything burned. But "Babylon," right? Like your song? They sing through the shit, right? You're fucked up on the river. Fucked up on the river but inside you still have hope!

(He plays tape.)

    CLYDE. *(Singing)* "The rivers of Babylon..." *(To Lucy, whispering)* That's all I know. *(To Jack)* "We sat down there..."
    JACK. "Where we sat down"!
    LUCY. "Where we sat down.

(CLYDE gestures for song, CONNIE joins in.)

    CONNIE. "But the wicked carried us away—"
    CLYDE. Come on, Jack, fuck it, forget it.

(JACK slightly emerges.)

    CLYDE. All right.. .that's better.
    JACK. It was just...
    CLYDE. I know.

(JACK comes out of the bathroom.)

    JACK. No one ever cooked for you.
    CONNIE. You did, though, it just.. .burned.

(CLYDE busies himself with coke.)

    CLYDE. It's gonna happen, just not right now. You're gonna cook, row in a boat, everything. It's all gonna happen. Right, Connie, everything? She loves you. We all love you and we will not give in to the dark forces. We will not give in to them. We move on. We lift our spirits.

(CLYDE crosses with coke for JACK. JACK does a line.
    CLYDE offers it to LUCY.)

Scene 24

(CLYDE and LUCY'S apartment. Later that night. They are all
    coked up.)

> LUCY. I think there's meth in this.
> CLYDE. What? No.

(JACK ENTERS from the bathroom.)

> JACK. She's OK.
> CLYDE. What's she doing?
> JACK. She's into the mirror.
> CLYDE. *(Regarding the line of coke.)* Yours.

(JACK does a line.)

> CLYDE. *(To no one.)* She's been in there a long time. *(To*
> LUCY, *offering a line of coke.)* Lucy?
>   JACK. She's looking in the mirror.
>   CLYDE. Yeah.
>   JACK. Looking into herself, she said.

LUCY. *(Doing the line.)* This is mine, too, right? I think there's meth in it.

CLYDE. What?

JACK. She said —

LUCY. I think there's —

CLYDE. It's just pure. Highgrade. The guy said.

LUCY. Who?

CLYDE. The guy, y'know, outside. The-Tip-to-Toe place guy.

LUCY. There's speed in it.

JACK. I'm gonna check on her. She's OK, though.

(LUCY does another line.)

CLYDE. We better not do more.

LUCY. I'm not.

CLYDE. Right. *(Doing it.)* Me too, after this. It's gone now, anyway, so...all done.

JACK. She's OK. She's looking in the mirror.

CLYDE. *(Beat.)* Who's looking?

JACK. Who? It's done?

CLYDE. Oh, yeah, Connie, you said that. Mirror on the wall. Yeah, gone — gone.

JACK. What?

CLYDE. She's coming out?

JACK. She knows what to do, she said.

LUCY. Who knows?

JACK. Her mind's made up.

LUCY. She's OK.

JACK. *(To no one.)* I'm gonna hit the hookah. *(To LUCY.)* Yeah. She'll come out. *(To no one.)* Take the edge down. *(To

Clyde.) **What?**
    CLYDE. Nothing. She coming out?
    JACK. Oh, Yeah. I think so. I'm gonna check.

(Buzzer. Instant paranoia.)

    LUCY. Who could it be?
    CLYDE. Don't move.

(CONNIE ENTERS.)

    CLYDE. Shhhh.
    JACK. They'll go away.
    CLYDE. Yeah.
    CONNIE. Who is it?
    LUCY. Could be anyone.
    CLYDE. We don't know.
    CONNIE. Should we ask?
    CLYDE. Don't ask.

(Buzzer.)

    CLYDE. Oh.
    LUCY. What?
    CLYDE. I forgot.
    LUCY. What?
    CLYDE. The cannoli.
    JACK. The cannoli?
    LUCY. The connoli?
    CONNIE. Who?

(Cell phone rings.)

JACK. Yours, right?

(CLYDE removes phone from pocket.)

CLYDE. Mine.

(They stare at it, phone stops.)

CLYDE. Restricted.
JACK. He'll leave.
CLYDE. *(To no one.)* Yes. *(To JACK.)* You think so?
LUCY. Why is the cannoli here?
CLYDE. Dessert.
LUCY. He came?
CLYDE. Maybe.
CONNIE. Who is he?
CLYDE. Someone's coming up the stairs.

(The anxiety intensifies.)

CONNIE. What?
CLYDE. He's in the building.
JACK. Someone let him in?
CLYDE. Someone's coming down the hall.
LUCY. Don't answer.
CLYDE. Someone's coming to the door. Put out the
lights.
JACK. The lights?
CLYDE. Put them out.

*(They put out the lights. Black. They tense, hiding in plain
   sight though it's dark onstage. Doorbell rings. Knocking.
   Pause.)*

  JACK. Oh, man...

(CLYDE tip toes to look out the peep hole. He returns.)

  CLYDE. They're gone.
  JACK. They?
  CLYDE. Him.
  JACK. It was the cannoli?
  CLYDE. Who else?
  LUCY. Put on the fucking lights!

(LUCY puts on a light.)

  LUCY. You wanted to totally fuck up a perfectly good time
with friends. Make it all about you!?
  CLYDE. I was going to be OK with it.
  LUCY. To totally embarrass me you fucking invited the
fucking cannoli!
  CLYDE. No, because, I've grown. I wanted to show I've
grown.
  LUCY. You are so fucked up. God. OK. OK. Forget it. OK.
OK?
  CONNIE. Yeah, uh-huh.
  JACK. Yeah. Ahem...hem. Ahem...hem...

(JACK'S nervous throat continues through the scene.)

CLYDE. I'm sorry...you're right, I'm fucked up.

LUCY. This didn't happen. OK. Just forget it. Forget you didn't fuck up the evening.

CLYDE. I wanted to be normal with the cannoli. I'll never be normal. I'm always going to be a baby. I'm always going to know you'll meet someone that has everything you want. You'll go with him because he's powerful and brilliant and charismatic. A megalomanic you can't resist. I drive a limo and go to night school. He'll be a genius at death or dessert or something else with class, someone so great he's a total shit to everyone, and they all love him. I'm only a stupid little ant opening car doors that has to be extra polite just to be liked by anyone!

JACK. Ahem...hem...hem...I like you.

CONNIE. Jack likes you.

CLYDE. I know Jack likes me!

CONNIE. He's your friend.

CLYDE. I know he's my fucking friend!!! OK? I know!

JACK. Don't, y'know, yell at her.

CLYDE. I'm sorry. I'm fucked up and she looks for some other life in some other person.

JACK. No. Ahem...ahem...hem...hem...ahem...hem...hem...

LUCY. That's what you think of me! I look!

CLYDE. I can't help it!

LUCY. You're right. You're a fucking baby! You're not good enough! Let's quit pretending!

(She EXITS to bedroom.)

CLYDE. Lucy! Don't. I know I'm fucked up.

(He EXITS after her.)

CLYDE. *(Offstage.)* Lucy. I'm sorry. Forgive me. I'm fucked up. I'm sorry.

(CLYDE pounds on bedroom door offstage.)

JACK. Ahem...hem... no, this is...
CLYDE. *(Offstage.)* I Love you. Lucy! Let me in, please. Please baby. Let me in. Lucy! LUCY!!!!!!

(CONNIE grabs the tape player, turns it on and hurries offstage with it.)

JACK. Ahem...hem...hem...ahem...hem...
CLYDE. *(Offstage.)* Fuck this fucking song.

(The tape player is hurled back onstage and crashes against the wall. It continues to play the "Babylon" lop, stops, skips, slows, etc. CONNIE hurriedly returns.)

CONNIE. Were going.
JACK. Ahem...hem...hem...ahem...hem...hem ahem...hem... hem...ahem...hem...
CONNIE. Jack. Let's leave.
JACK. Ahem...hem...hem...ahem...hem...hem ahem...hem... hem...ahem...
CONNIE. Jack. Let's go.

(Gets coats, takes charge. Pounding offstage.)

JACK. Ahem...hem...hem...ahem...hem...

(CONNIE and JACK EXIT. CLYDE wails and pleads.)

CLYDE. *(Offstage.)* Lucy! Ohhhhh. Lucy! Please! God! I'm fucked up! I'm totally fucked up!

LUCY. *(Offstage.)* Go the fuck away!

CLYDE. *(Offstage.)* Fucked up! Please, please, please... open the door! Lucy!

(Sound of bedroom door getting kicked in.)

LUCY. *(Offstage.)* Get the fuck out! Get the fuck out!

(CLYDE ENTERS the room. Distraught. Sits.)

CLYDE. Fuck...fuck...fuck...

(LUCY ENTERS. CLYDE stands, on verge of emotional breakdown. LUCY observes him.)

CLYDE. *(Unable to look at her.)* I'm sorry. I'm sorry. I wouldn't hurt you. I'm sorry.

(She picks up the tape player. Tries but can't succeed in turning it off. After a moment...)

LUCY. It won't stop.

CLYDE. Can I see? ...Lucy?

(He takes it. Fails to stop it. Puts it on the floor. Stomps on it. It stops. She puts a hand on him. He turns to bury himself in her.)

CLYDE. I don't want to lose you.

Scene 25

(CONNIE'S apartment. JACK and CONNIE enter.)

JACK . Wow. Y'know? I mean...that was...
CONNIE. My nerves are rattling.
JACK. Maybe I should go.
CONNIE. No!
JACK. OK!
CONNIE. You could hold me.
JACK. OK.

(They are holding on tight in silence.)

CONNIE. My heart's pounding.
JACK. I know.

(They hold one another in silence.)

CONNIE. Oh, ah.
JACK. OK?
CONNIE. Yeah. I don't want it ever to be like that.
JACK. No. Uh-uh...
CONNIE. That's why I'm standing here with you.
JACK. This feels good now. Better.
CONNIE. Jack?
JACK. Yeah?
CONNIE. If you took me —

JACK. Huh?
CONNIE. Took me.
JACK. Took you?
CONNIE. Over power me.
JACK. Oh.

(They remain holding each other in silence.)

CONNIE. That's your heart.
JACK. Yeah.
CONNIE. Racing.
JACK. Yeah.

(They hold each other in silence.)

CONNIE. I pictured the first time by the lake, but maybe it should just be now. I pictured grass by a lake but it could be now — if you overpower me.
JACK. Over power you?
CONNIE. Force me, in a way —
JACK. Oh.
CONNIE. Make me.
JACK. Make you?
CONNIE. Hold me down, and take off my clothes, and don't hurt me, but overcome me.
JACK. Yeah?
CONNIE. You think you can?
JACK. Yeah.
CONNIE. You can?
JACK. Yeah.
CONNIE. Will you?

JACK. Yeah.
CONNIE. OK.

(She lets go a little.)

JACK. I really like you.
CONNIE. I know.
JACK. OK.
CONNIE. Don't hurt me. Overpower me.

(He backs her to the bed. She looks a little frightened. He releases her.)

JACK. You alright?
CONNIE. You're strong.
JACK. Swimming practice.
CONNIE. You're good at it. I'll bet.
JACK. Getting there.
CONNIE. Come on...
JACK. Yeah.

(He makes a move and she makes a slight move of resistance.)

CONNIE. I want you...to take me. *(She smiles, breathlessly.)* Come on...take me.

(He moves her forcefully to the bed. She wraps herself around him.)

Scene 26

(Swim deck.)

CLYDE. That's it, pull the water to you...let it go...pull the water and let go. Let everything flow...Good, see, you're swimming. There is no deep end. You're at the deep end but there is no deep end. That's right. Good. Good. I'm coming in. I'm gonna do some laps. Great. Great. *(Swimming)* Oh, yeah. Oh, yeah. Oh, yeah.

Scene 27

(Lake. JACK rows CONNIE in a boat.)

JACK. OK?
CONNIE. Yeah.
JACK. Don't worry.
CONNIE. OK.
JACK. I'm a good swimmer.
CONNIE. I knew you would be. When we talked about summer. You'd be good at swimming.
JACK. I am for you. *(They kiss.)*
CONNIE. That you'd be good.
JACK. I am for you.

(JACK rows them on.)

THE END

The Clean House
By Sarah Ruhl
2005 Pulitzer Prize Finalist

This extraordinary new play by an exciting new voice in the American drama was runner-up for the Pulitzer Prize. The play takes place in what the author describes as "metaphysical Connecticut", mostly in the home of a married couple who are both doctors. They have hired a housekeeper named Matilde, an aspiring comedian from Brazil who's more interested in coming up with the perfect joke than in house-cleaning. Lane, the lady of the house, has an eccentric sister named Virginia who's just nuts about house-cleaning. She and Matilde become fast friends, and Virginia takes over the cleaning while Matilde works on her jokes. Trouble comes when Lane's husband Charles reveals that he has found his soul mate, or "bashert" in a cancer patient named Anna, on whom he has operated. The actors who play Charles and Anna also play Matilde's parents in a series of dream-like memories, as we learn the story about how they literally killed each other with laughter, giving new meaning to the phrase, "I almost died laughing." This theatrical and wildly funny play is a whimsical and poignant look at class, comedy and the true nature of love. 1m, 4f (#6266)

"Fresh, funny ... a memorable play, imbued with a somehow comforting philosophy: that the messes and disappointments of life are as much a part of its beauty as romantic love and chocolate ice cream, and a perfect punch line can be as sublime as the most wrenchingly lovely aria." — *NY Times*

See the Samuel French website at **samuelfrench.com** or our **Basic Catalogue of Plays and Musicals** for more information.